HOME PLANET

poems

Tom Henighan

THE GOLDEN DOG PRESS
OTTAWA—CANADA—1994

ISBN 0-919614-57-4

Canadian Cataloguing in Publication Data
Henighan, Tom
        Home Planet

Poems.
ISBN 0-919614-57-4

        I. Title

PS8565.E582H65   C811'.54   C94-900606-8
PR9199.3.H46H65 1994

Printed and bound in Canada.

HOME PLANET

FOR MARILYN

Also by Tom Henighan

Brave New Universe: Testing the Value of Science in Society, 1980

Natural Space in Literature, 1982

Tourists from Algol (stories), 1983

The Well of Time (novel), 1988

Strange Attractors (stories), 1992

CONTENTS

I   FIRST CONTACT

OPENING THE COTTAGE

Memory revives
after winter,
each cabin is roughly assembled —
men rig the pumps,
the women improvise:
chairs are dusted, grouped,
tables dragged from sleep
antique bowling pins
can make a display . . .
spare cushions,
aunt's crude oils, the family gushers,
fine on the long porch.

The tidy docks, the gathered
lives —
as if nature,
in pitiless beauty,
required this slack homage
to spring, when a human
beginning in innocence
turns round to discover
lives lost in thickets,
a family so rooted in custom
it is alien.

The story goes
that one child of a settler
choked by the old ways
pushed on to the city, taught school,
cornered markets, grew rich.
A story without surprises
except in the dark hours
when securities failed
each aunt folded her lace up and cried,
husbands got drunk, married cancer,
mothers clutched sons with their hurt hands.

Meanwhile the cottage stayed heaven
though the last bear was shot and petrol
leaked into the lake,
newcomers complained about the noise.
(A body can be dreamless
in the best sleeping porch
between Renfrew and Bay Street).

So rooms filled up with junk
the barbecues were active
daughters flew weeping home
sons grunted a rivalry of risk
staked everything on the motto
"mind your own business."
While their wives, each captured princess,
paced through quick years to the future,
the boathouse groaned with craft
that could circle forever
without touching bottom.

Up long muddied trails
through the bare woods
cars gouge the bush,
hauling tools
of resistance,
disgorging traces —
a beach ball, a basket, an old shoe. . .

More is lost.
What fells the tamed trees
holds the heart without song —
until the eye,
made perfect by regret,
finds grace in the smoky air
the unwilling sun,
sees glacial waters stir
in arterial darkness
under the leaf-tangled snow.

And rarely
the woods burst forth
with speech of hidden tongues,
the owl's cry
a trembling at the roots,
rain on needled tufts,
or cold dawns
whose light fires the blood—
human moments
raw with a god's rage
to catch the living echo,
the wild body flung over
its earthly pitfalls
of time, accustomed comforts.

We move, as in circles of light,
where rough thickets dance
and beat like shameless memories
against the seasoned heart.

SLEEPING BEAUTY

You can't help it if you sleep all day.
Light weasels into the room with the true
Pre-Raphaelite unreality. There you are
With that drizzle of hair breast-tethered,
Asleep. In a minute you'll yawn,
Roll your eyes as if you were coming
And go nowhere. Or ask if I want breakfast
(Lunch dishes just washed). Friends
Might say: this is common law but not
Common sense. They forget at two
In the morning you'll be throwing
A tantrum, questions about Bartok.
Sleep out your time, non-sequitur.

CLARK KENT IN OLD AGE

Weightless, inside this mortal suit,
the tonnage of years on a stick,
I clutch at each clue to the old life.
An orphan of suffering, in search of
miraculous time, lovely muscle
of wish become flesh, but the changes!
One arm and a stiffly drawn head
twisted upward, I stumble . . .
They help me as much as they can,
their regret green as once their envy
grew, green as Krypton—a slow rot
begins in the brain, in the crotch,
superlatives die before the rest.
Only comic? Never mind if the elegy's
coined for your cat, or your goldfish—
you imagined it all, Lear too, and
Samson. Jobbers and sad old men
as well as princes of royal blood
hire fools or are aped
by their lackeys. Die, decline,
fade away or are forgotten.
Hero and clown all at once,
Unreal but never spurious,
I carried what I could
of your first lust for story.
Consider at least your own joy,
how the colours moved in your mind
as you dodged through backyards
where not even your X-ray eyes
could see the rubble of your own childhood.
And if you don't pity me
pity at least what your mirror shows
of what you might have been
without fear and the perils
of too much gravity.

PAOLO TO FRANCESCA

DANTE: CANTO V, LIMBO:
The Second Circle: the carnal

One millisecond behind me,
I sense your word,
feathering time's arrow,

making the void sing
with hidden syllables
I might have answered

if we hadn't parted
at the common nexus
of all luckless lovers.

Probabilities flow
as they must —

We are whirled
time out of mind

as love blows us
shrilly apart.

If with cruel skill
we rode the charged waves
back to that first blinding wish,

falling from dark space
to the room
where our text became flesh,

hand locked in hand
from this circle
we'd pull down the sun,

break the moon's spell
on every yearning eye

hurl passionate tides
across the unboundaried earth

and drown the book of the world
in the tears of its maker.

THE GARDENING MONK

It's my birthday.
In the next room, as if for the first time,
my wife is reading Genesis.
I've just unpeeled myself from nine innings
of little men hitting a mostly invisible ball
past other little men. The National League
has become the National . . . strikes, promises, threats.
The announcer lends bonhomie sadness.
Years pass, the news never changes.
"From which of the twelve tribes was Christ descended?"
shouts my wife. "The Cincinnati Reds," I reply,
tired of testaments and stolen bases.

Outside, it's raining. My children are far away.
The cats want in. The dogs don't want to be put out.
Who'd believe that the monk in the basement
could be setting out rows for a garden.
Unearthing grave objects while the household
drifts toward one sleep or another —
arrowheads, pottery, a few poems —
laid secretly down in the root cellar
against winter, too many distractions,
or harvested lightly in dreams.

THE SORCERESS

Lady on her dream farm spinning
gold from straw,
behind the frilly trellis
cooking up something nice
until all the dogs of the country
howl for a lick
of the fat gingerbread
of her imagination.
Oven chock full of their mother's
fancies, her kids cut lovely shapes
in the mouth-watering day
while the man cleans up the yard
coming in just in time
to taste her cookies
it's rich, such a life,
and a monthly check from fairy land
pays for it all.

But when you meet her at last
and she lies down
spooning words
until the dogs tear chains,
taste everything in moderation.
Though you fly
the sweetest veins
from pleasure to pleasure
never never land
in that room stuffed full
of candied cobs,
in the well rigged with mirrors —
there, with starved magic
she lays it on thick:
Old Sugar Daddy,
guard your private sleep
or those scampering hands
will repeat on you
the frosting of nightmare.

FIRST CONTACT

An alien invites my wife to a cheap motel.
He is almost human, except for the unblinking eyes.
She drinks, brazen as Barbarella, while he loops
wishes ever closer around her careless mind.
Gently, as one lately fallen to earth,
he divines she is willing to stay,
so long as the proper decorum excuses
her spirit of adventure from all earthly shame.
Half-dressed, they lie in bed; he enfolds her
willingness in wings,
she senses a rare music in his muttered charms.
Nakedness achieved, he is like any other,
until the sudden leap inside her
restores the wild forbidden contact lost
when the Sons of God left the Daughters of Men
to their husbands.

Always some plot fleshing out
the domestic strain
with an older mystery,
always the alien heart
surprising itself
in a human mirror, sudden with light.
A lost heaven hangs on my words,
even so, I betray my story
with sadly unblinking eyes.

DOMESTIC MYSTERIES

Stacked dishes, floor swept clean,
the children aimed at sleep,
here's time to take in hand
the resolutions of years or of hours,
languages to learn and books to read—
sewing and weaving and puttering around
in the attics and sheds of the mind;
or the body restored by contortion.

Yet when the rose-red of the lampshade nuzzles
the corner darkness, the moon slides up
the window, and bright carpet mazes
point inward, our thoughts shift and unravel,
we sink far below the horizon
of imminent discipline
and offer a quiet mind to domestic mysteries.

Woodface and bookspine, the tick of the clock,
and the pulse slowing down till it penetrates
dust, metal, polish
composing all this fretwork
of white lace to a clear
declaration. This is your order,
a fugue of uncommon things—
green glass, Pullman couch
ripe Moorcroft, a Beluchi
with just the right note
of the threadbare,
as if some dear plush
carpet would
bankrupt sense
or fail underfoot
your true amateur's
vision.

I see what a chauvinist you are
of beauty, as well as pain,
you insist we inhabit
this rare diorama
that enshrines brooding peace
where once we paid tribute
with shattered treasures
to the mess of our lives.

Angles shift, pure disorder's relentless,
but tonight the fire heartens,
the stairway curves up to heaven,
plants root down deeper in place,
and our tiny chipped Buddha,
smiles calmly, presiding with grace
from old grooves of unfailing attachment.

THAT SUMMER

That summer you worked in town
the arguing stopped.
Fields fallowed over,
hard apples dropped
from slack trees
on the tangled bush.
The barn yawned
when the wind made up
its bedding of hay,
old bales paunched out
forever unsold
in the dark loft.
With you in the city
the country hung
in a slippery silence,
and only in retrospect
did your love groans tumble in
from whatever motel it was
to rattle my late sleep
like summer thunder.

SHE ANNOUNCES . . .

Her voice, husky with love,
for its own speech, for all things,
like a quiet bell chiming
in the silence of the studio
as shadows genuflect
what saint's mock-up
of time without death
can match the diamond heart
of such perfection?

In scales beyond distraction,
a quantum of miracle:
to be in more than one place
at the same time.
The holy hardware sings,
we know her trajectory's heaven.

But not an irrational heaven,
where longing multiplies itself
by the square root of minus one:
here confusion is wiped from the mind,
bright cones and whirling spools
confirm a void
beautiful as a monastery
forgotten by the terror of God.

She speaks out of gravity
her words fly, unearthly,
they climb upon a thread
of human music, weightless,
search deep in the dark core
of unimagined stars,
in far space
wake spirals of quiet time
curved lightly
as delicate ears.

EX PARTE

this child
       who presumed to grow up
          in our bed
      in the kitchen
slaps everything
to order
     hides
the diamond of her motion
        in repose.
tagging along
       in hope
secrets would drop from the blue
     study
her madonna self creeps into,
             for years
squeezing the air
    for my trouble
bamboozled
    with love
as she calls her persistence,
          I knocked on doors
was handed
    a menu, a timetable, or a towel,
pretending to read the newspaper,
    snapped at the loose ends
of her disguise
    without unmasking it.

               flat on her back
heaving children
               into the world
as locked as a sub
               she's asleep
in her element
                       can't fathom
        why I murmur
               for knowledge
        even the thud
of my body
               releasing itself
in her arms
        always signals beyond—
a blind spy
        in the wake
of her wonder.

A SIGHT

gutted by all those failures
he struck a light so that his body
lifted its frail shell above the shadows.

we'd seen through him for so long
the miracle was transparent.
"It's a Christly life," he said,
and meant it.

GENRE FICTION

When I was married to Madame Maigret
I found my way back to the tidy apartment,
trouble snapped at my heels, unrelenting.
Pursuing the false gait of the fatally indolent,
I outwalked aristocrats fresh from their baths.
Weekends off season I flew to the Midi —
stepped across bodies entwined on the beaches;
or lost in that country forgotten by tourists,
discovered the trite patrimonial snares.
Experience soured me; but even that knowledge
I wore like a medal; self-reproach was my burden:
not for the *patron* to whine about corruption,
tight-lipped, I faced the worst: the pipe helped,
a small prop pointing to the inner fire.
Even so, in a life without mystery,
on bleak streets, in a drizzle of circumstance,
one case became another, until home-bound,
exhausted, fed up, always hungry,
I shed each adventure as I wiped off my shoes.
Happiness has no solution.
Enlisted by habit, to taste sombre love —
a plump bird in the oven and a good wine decanted,
I settled in bed, heard the wind at the shutters,
as a voice whispered out of the darkness: "Just sleep".

SPEECH AND SILENCE

The universe is always hungry.
No beam of pity
in the darkness of time.
The deep wolf roars so loud
swallowing stars and people
gods and history,
all to no purpose —
you can't even whistle.
That's the worst of being human
puffed up with words —
God, *love* and *death* —
those frightening bridges
a thousand feet high,
no abyss without a name.
One thing feeds on another,
it's as simple as that.
Speech leaves you in sight
of insatiable hungers.
Silence does the same.

II DISTANT VIEWING

Ixion

Lost country, far north of every hope.
The fields make a riot of grass and sunlight.
You've gone yet you move in dark hollows,
lifting white arms to pull me close to roots.
Here I'm tangled, bound underneath the blue sky
just dissolving, melting into the memory of a shape
that once seemed fixed in my mind like a wheel of ice.

Midsummer Evening

All the trees in new consciousness
breathed and lifted their branches —
a green choir pitched in voiceless song.
The sun fell slowly as the moon rose,
shadows lightened, speckled with rare fire
of unseen elements.
The transparent earth revealed itself,
mirroring quiet depths of the deep sky.

Dionysus

Thinking of you, I tear the clothes from my body.
Beat my arms and legs on the pines and rough grass.
Drink red wine and stagger down into black mud.
Terrified animals shrink from me. I howl, sinking fast,
for the reeds cannot hold me. The last thing I see
is the white moon like a skull in the blurred sky.

Postcard from the Second World

Fallen from line and color
I hang in the meshes of words
unable to speak because a song
beats strongly in my captive heart.
I stretch out my fist, smash my way
into the first world, blinded by old apparitions,
pure visions we used to call
"red," "green," or "yellow."
In the first world we see and are silent.

Wind-spirit

It is what takes the trees beyond themselves,
breaking boundaries of air,
the breath of gods on the nape of the grass,
the shifting of leaves, the wild pollen in flight.
It is the swirl of your dress among larkspur and milkweed,
the magical movement of your hair.

Scarred Landscape

The air's acid light. The smell of brimstone.
Fields gone ragged with nettles and rank grass.
Someone has opened a small vent to hell. Listen!
On this windless day you can almost hear the laughter
of the damned.

Indian Summer

Stones fly. Voices break like glass.
The lying drums will compose a mystery
made of fear and feathers. Sirens, laughter.
Bulldozers gouging the Mother.
Wounded earth dies by decree, a failed bargain.
A child howls in a forgotten language
manhandled by the shadow of a stark tower.

Winter

Branches punctuate a blank page of snow.
Scrawled lines stretch to sheer points,
bearing white stars like new frost. Period. End of the world.
New beginning.

Winter II

Bare branches make a crucifixion of sunset.
The body of God has risen from the earth,
cracking cruel stones, moving toward us like a glacier
holy with light.

Thunderstorm

Earth roars in the whirlwind, terrified of its own voice,
blinded by an instant's light. We are meant to look up,
to fix on the wild sky. Some god is making love in the furrows.

III   DOUBLE VISION

PENGUINS

By all odds upside down
the penguins live in peace,
blackmasked good guys
who play on the stoop of the world,
like automatons
shuttled from space
to amuse us they dally,
poor natives disguised as colonials
stuck on one mate
growing warmblooded slowly
worn down to a brushcut
bob up
after eight months at sea,
outlasting Byrd, half-fish
and almost as real
as Coleridge's salt,
hurled into straits
by the ultrasonic bellows
of a world unmoored —

yet charting
the reverse English of earth's deep motion.
Quite unimaginable
their amphibious sorrows,
joys born due south
of all poetry.

Now pulled back suddenly —
I remember,
an ocean away,
little girls in a bookstore
to see the penguins
and disappointed to find
they were only books.

TV WAR

The living child
hammering on the glass
touched me, and died.

I laid
the ghost of her humanity
between commercials.

THE ACADEMY OF GOOD CAUSES

A quiet day
at the academy of good causes.
They castrated a fifty-year-old rake
who envisioned some unbelievable beauty
in the crude framework of a ten-second leer,

— drew and quartered
a lover of raw life
whose soul was offended
when they planted a stray fetus
in Mrs. Parkinson's brain.

And for good measure hanged a smoker
who was groping for some matches
to light a memorial candle
in the skull of an old-fashioned humanist.

HOMILY

We live on a strange planet,
addicted to machinery and odd-coloured toothpaste,
ready faces disguising the shy animals inside us, who peer out,
occasionally baffled, as a mouth tightens, a smile breaks,
a life's work rots like cheese.

We stand motionless, yet a moving stairway
propels us at lunatic speed toward a blank sky.
Nothing happens. Everything is threatened.

Wriggling in and out of costumes,
we catch glimpses of each other,
pretending to be children, robots, stars,
burying trinkets, planning to live forever,
while the sour-eyed invisible devil who rules us,
cuts away at our flesh.

Infected by language
our skulls grow oracular
brave sentences gnaw at the darkness
explode needle light, or
sink everything out of sight
in a mineshaft of reveries
each one singular and foolish
as a mantra.

While we murder our best dreams
the old earth, like a gnarled peasant,
cheers unthinkable weathers
through each cycle and season
nudges us toward a backyard wisdom
that anchors our wild flights
on the toughest tether.

BONSAI MAN

The bonsai man has made a tiny forest:
wise tough pines and ailanthus,
lean poplars and sturdy maples,
amazing oaks and elms not in dutch,
suitably placed and spaced,
with fine grass neat as a combtooth,
all manner of shrubbery, wildflowers,
which, magnified, leap into colour,
and insects whose images dance in the mirror
that lies in the miniature toolbox
at the edge of the dwarf woods.

Now the bonsai man is contriving a little family
that will walk in the forest and sing and play croquet
in the clearing two inches from the left edge.
It may take him centuries to complete them,
for he works very slowly, being himself
only two feet tall and left-handed,
relying on nothing but patience and quick shears.

POSTCARD OF A JAPANESE WOODCUT

KATSHUSHIKA TAITO'S WOODCUT:
"A Carp Leaping in a Pool"

The carp climbs to the blue air.
You wake alert in the possible room,
Breakfast floats after the alarm.
The wind is terse today, but warm.
Solicitude measures you a chair.
The codes are known, so much to tell
With headache gone, libido well.
Will it be leaf, or stone, or sky,
The colour of time, the colour of skin?
The carp climbs to the blue air,
A rage appointed for each fin.

The sun you woke to snaps at ten,
Your page is blanker than the glare.
The streets flush truth at every coil,
Drooping children perk at dogs,
Invisible mailmen move like clocks.

The carp climbs to the blue air.
Your fingers drown a major key,
The sculptured world you rose to catch
Is sliding skyward toward the sea.

You're up and heading for the door
As borders whistle down to blur,
In distances the day could spare
The carp climbs to the blue air.

POINTING NORTH

(after Christian Morgenstern)

McNulty's weird — he points his head
Northward when he lies in bed,

Avoiding south and east and west,
Just managing to get some rest.

A foolish trick, his shrink declares,
To catch the compass unawares.

Irrational, suggest the scholars,
As they recycle truth for dollars.

All this is manifest to seers
Who chart blue planets in arrears,

And poets, turning words on dimes
Drive nonsense home with backseat rhymes.

McNulty, not to be outdone,
Lies down beneath the midnight sun

A stranger in a common dream,
He hears the polar foxes scream.

THE GREAT COMEDIANS

(for Robert Zend)

The great comedians fall, one by one,
into a surprising cosmos.
Galaxies roar out of sight;
somewhere near Vegas, through a desert of spaces,
all jokes circle round.
Heisenberg's agents are weeping
but gravity endures — the eternal gravity of humour —
the pratfall, the banana peel, the pie in the face —
and it's Chaplin, so nakedly manifold, one foot
in a whirlpool,
whose precarious spirals astound us
before he disappears.

O strange attractors, peering out of chaos,
while Harpo holds time on a string,
forever, at the flip of a coin, Harold Lloyd will recover
pure silence; Stan Laurel beside himself
in the commotions of laughter,
Lenny Bruce embracing death
with his spiral arms.

How artfully they bow and vanish!
Mr. Fields will allow, sir,
that the Great White Way dawdles
at the edge of oblivion —
queer quasars, real howlers,
space expanding to shrink us.

And worse than Woody Allen's fears
no universal dance, but dense
fires winking into darkness,
black holes in a tired script
of stars.

(Yet when Keaton is called back
nothing human is laughable —

and even the supernovas
balance a moment in the love
that urges a small man
with sheer grace
from one fall to another).

CIRCUS

Sadness of circuses
        trombones spit sawdust
Wrong kind of elephant
        big bland scum monsters
Disguised slugs
        and Stromboli hanged
In a yellow shirt
        twirls in our dreams.
Webbed aisles pink candy sick
        tasting of cod-liver oil,
Gargantua unmated
        pendulum fugitives
With fascisti names,
        oppressed by umbrellas
Circles and space.
        Tip of a whip
To the sleeping lions:
        "claw in great red strips,"
Instead
        5000 feet above the fright in your throat
The girl notches the bar
        between her thighs,
Drumbeats of the congenital
        war. Fools roar.
Grandmother's fading away . . .

DISCOVERY

Dreams of Saturn clear.
Long walls fine as lime,
boot-tapped corridors,
silence in the dome
except for the echo of those
or stopped, the slow clock.
Under the glass sphere lights
snap to refractory rhythms,
through an outside innocent
of poisons, in the white
sunlight we must have imagined,
the ships like paper boats —
fragile, hovering.

If there was a mission
we had forgotten already,

our minds on bearings
sliding toward some destiny
across obstructions
tripping the springs until
doors open and close.

Peace is the shape we draw,
a golden crew who have landed
in what they own, happy,
but folded aside inside
our certainty, bent down
to some disturbing trace
or spider trail, colours
missing from the spectrum,
an imagined whisper . . .

VISITATION

They landed one night and I loved them,
bright shapes in the dark woods,
speaking my language with tongues
that set fire to my heart.
I remembered the roar of Atlantis,
the pyramids seen from the sky.
I was naked, they touched me with tentacled arms
and I slept as we hovered in black space
so peaceful. Icy spires gleamed
when they told me of God,
who would come in a great shining ship
to destroy all the wicked.
We departed the galaxy wrapped in
orange light, never once did I think
of my wife, of my mother. I was glad
to give up my job, to travel in those
other worlds. They night they came
the baby cried, dinner was late,
there was insurance to pay and no money
in the bank. The last thing I saw was
the stroller with the broken wheel,
beside the mailbox. I just closed my eyes.
A blue steel cylinder swept me away.
I looked at the earth hanging bright
as a Christmas ornament. I was happy.

Now I'm home again; it's like a dream.
Everything is somehow wrong here.
The neighbours speak blasphemy, mock me.
The house shrinks and darkens,
these rough walls peel strangely, like skin.
I run to the woodshed and hide.
A light shivers blue in my veins.
Stars roar and, shuddering, fall.

44

ON THAT PLANET

On that planet
steep mountains crack
the mind entertains
its destruction.

On that planet
unleavened hope
a dry throat announces
sad routes, lost wonder.

On that planet
power weighs the heart
a fist crashes down
like a new birth.

On that planet
the rich will recover
each day a tithe
of their charity.

On that planet
long married couples
slowly poisoned by memories
as their images kiss.

On that planet
bleak age exacts
the child's buried wish.

On that planet,
its atmosphere torn,
what leaks into space
is a cry.

SPACE OPERA

Lovable mind monsters
numbered tin or stuffed
we make Oz between stars
plotting adventures
in the illusion
they might happen.

Not dreamland
dashed off
as the future
invading our heads
with a story
which, for all its beauty,
can never be told,
but the life of a princess,
a hero, old wars
afflicting the galaxy
less than a sneeze, us
somewhat more,
for the fever's in us:
we survive it
gathering strands of our deepest spaces
to discover
that moment between verbs and pictures
when the princess nods
the lights in the palace flicker
the planet stops.

Then enter white noise and dark silence —
to escape it we zoom out
rewinding a gossamer foolishness,
bold youths and sly robots,
who confound the stentorian villain,
never dream that his mask hides
the bald prima donna:
she who poisons the popcorn
of time, space and memory,

and sings behind the gorgeous soundtrack
the love-death
of every simple pleasure.

A LITTLE NUMBER BY VIVALDI

This man, this
   redheaded Italian, this
   priest of musicians,
who lost to the bombers in Dresden
   when the world had run out of
carnivals,
   manuscripts enough to paper
the mouths of warmongers everywhere,
   a cupful only
in his Adriatic, though more
   than we might imagine
sitting up nights
   the four seasons
of three centuries —
   You can almost see him score
   page after page
the brave bullseyes of joy
his music through the mind starts
   plunking
         strings that whip the curd
   off living
   darkeyed kids
   with kernel faces
jump through upside down gondolas
   set lagoons in storm
blowing out palazzi —
   cobwebbed silences be damned
when this priest gets cricket palsy —
   think of the *ospedale*
Venice,
   where girls skipped through his skills,
   magnificats
out of back alley terrors
   (reread Casanova)
the filthy sheeting traded in
   for clean counterpoint.

Winters no perfumes could warm
    hot after practice
violas screeched to the high ceilings,
    if that doesn't certify
patience, what does?

They learned the values well
    — plain and decorated —
for fun or maybe out of fright
    il prete rosso would frown
    and dreamed of
sliding down stairs
    onto doorsteps
    poor orphans
fleshed out with graces
    concerted bodies played

    every spring at least
    (in white cocoons)
melodies of the Red Admiral —
    what they could do
    their townsmen quick to sight read
knew,
    and visitors were ravished.
    "There is no instrument so big
    as to intimidate them,"
    one observed,
more innocent than they became,
I hope.
    But they were pure enough to bend
                    the tinnest ear
    to music
    & only the blind could fail
to hear
    that dancing bright as festivals
    for which the old man twirled out
a dozen pieces
    beating time

as Venice fell around them
like a golden quilt.
    Probably he remembered that
in Vienna,
    where he died,
    the public as usual
    forgetting
violins rusted out of mind
tunes imprisoned in print
    useless as old scorecards,
    girls gone crabbed and flat —
but where there's art
    there's hope
leads everywhere
out of speakers
such talent years feed back
    ghost girls living on
sound
    haunt Brooklyn and Zurich
    through the long nights
his kind of happiness makes good.
    Listen:

IV   GHOST STONES

NOTE

In *America B.C.* and elsewhere, Dr. Barry Fell has argued that
North America was first settled by Celtic and North African
peoples who set up stone monuments connected with their re-
ligion of seasonal nature and the stars. Other specialists doubt
this theory and see the stones as merely "natural' outcrop-
pings, accidentally marked in the course of the centuries.

(1) The Children

Babies in deep swell of cursive
riding waves west
breasting oil slick of tankers
nuke subs and dolphins at bay.
like figures from old maps
the putti run rockwise
to windward, steer their rubbery
bodies, alert to the seasons,
toward a new world.

They scratch signs upon stone,
then vanish at first light
float off the edge of the mind
strung out like syllables
bawling skyward those infants
of another odour sniff
the big bland spaces,
leapfrog centuries
to plant their brave rumps on the moon
chasing golfballs —
only a few lines on their primped
skin, mouths full of jellybeans —
let's cancel the arts and all poetry
enjoying this second childhood
play with our guns while we still
get them up,
kill the natives.

Out of the long ships of Tarshish
schooled in old alphabets
infants of new speech
break lightning on plow-struck
stones, make sense of this
hacked land,
initialed by glaciers
and bears to no purpose
groomed by the elements,

deep roots of the world tree
survive us
like our most denuded
first-born selves.

(2) Landlocked

Steel plows turn up savage bones
old compasses marry dimensions
in darkness the starved herds
bolt a surplus of time
carved into rock
all around this astonishing rubble
of plastic and painted tires
one-armed dolls, pink flamingoes
& little black boys with poses
dismembering memory.

Things here go downhill
a little slower
than anywhere else,
cows chomp at fallen fences
could care less what makes the grass grow,
barn roofs a drizzle of rust
the dogs all covered in plywood.
Colonel Sanders, a white worm
at the windows, beckons,
and out of the woods rise the beasts,
gods and men, violent spears
at their thighs —
though, in sight of the women,
they vanish,
as shacks multiply like unpaid bills,
and Biz Froats ups from his tractor, swearing:
"The only hope for this country's some outside
investment. The farmer can't make a living anymore,
but Hydro's promised us a nuclear station
and you goddamn well better believe
that we need it."

(3) Mahair-Mabona*

This is the mother
drowned deep in sorrow
stretched under winter
a boulder, a shadow
a tangle of bush
crone of the streetcorners
losing her buspass
in the filthy snow
forfeiting pensions
tightening the tether
on her wayward sons
peering out from a mask
of powder and wrinkles
in a cracked voice
cautioning
sick with complaints
about the weather
wearing out patience
her truculent whining
repeated forever
in the same words
in the same tone
in the same room
carried by ship
from country to country
the forceps of moonlight
compel her,
she waits in the car
or visiting church
is helped up the stairs
in diamonds or rags
binding her daughters
who lie trapped in birth

---

*literally, "mother of heroes." The Celtic mother goddess, tributes to whom (according to Barry Fell) are found in certain North American inscriptions.

trussed up and stirruped
like victims
tempting a wayward sunlight
to strike the familiar
uncertain bargains
of pleasure and death.

(4) Mabo–Mabona*

He is the young strong god.
Eaten up by the cameras
and the wishes of women
he learns to take sail
in the root-cellared sea.
Words hang like lures
in the scrolled darkness
soft tides of speech
draw him down in pursuit
of the golden beaches,
the shining sea-caves.
When he sleeps he can almost
touch the blue spars
of wrecks whose antennae
stretch through jungles
of coral to the foot of
the oil rigs.

He follows the wounded whales
to polluted embankments,
skylines of cities
tremble like
graphs of mirages,
the outskirts harbour
grim shacks of the poor
where garbage
picked at by children
recycles with famine.
He dies in the mountains.
The earth roars and he changes.
Under the evergreens, bones,
in the shining riverbed, bones,
bones on the steaming prairies —
his dreams an equator of journeys.

---

*Celtic god of youth (related to the Greco-Roman Apollo), whose
altars, according to Fell, are to be found occasionally in North America.

(5) Harvest Supper

Everybody quiet. It's time to clean out the ghosts
with the same spells that invoked them.
Uncork the dry red, slash leaves from that tangle
hiding the big stones. Pay no mind to old writing
scratched under moss. Seize the wild vine,
to be draped around the girl who looks best
in least. Take the corn ears and roast them
and let fly with butter and salt, and no lewd jokes
when there's time for right action tomorrow.

This is an honest-to-god holiday, put down the chainsaw
climb off the tractor, rest your butt on the earth.
Let the cows graze ribboned with light near the house.
Let everything happen, nobody forcing the issue.
There's the fire, clean burning, so toss in the rubbish,
old newspapers full of war PR profit
(but save the obits, which make good reading in retirement).
Save the reviews discreetly for the back house;
toss in the mortgage, we're moving out pronto,
heading off to the boondocks where the spirit so lightly
slips anchor.

Fuel the fire higher with debts and compulsions,
loud static to foul up the peace of the day,
when nothing's enough you caress breast and bottle,
your head wallows, your hands are more than idle.
Burn every injunction, all platitudes gratis
from MPs in hock to the language, then stand back
to avoid inhaling the stink of your virtue.
Look, it's OK, your liver can live with the strain.
The omens are right for a boozeup,
turn handsprings or stagger erect to the bushes.
If the lady can stand you, she's worth all the trouble.
You'll make it, for once, without silly palaver.

With sharp eyes find shapes in the clearings,
A long-haired ex-hippie with small cloven feet
who makes a racket when he's stoned, which is always.
He gave up his guitar long ago for a flute,
patron of the first comers, the early risers,
who settled down in happy places
and said fuck the snow, there's fire in our guts —
they blessed the uncertain springs, the darkest water.

Watch out for the messenger,
wise guy with a pickup, the old crook,
rides over to tell you the good news,
you won the lottery — and there's only one small catch!

Or him with the green thumb, the home brew,
who covers your house with prismatic vines.
When the door jams — in case of fire — go back to the orgy
he's conjured in the rec room you never built.

Then meet the lady champion, dead-shot with the bright bow,
you blink only once at her beauty.
Her aim has nothing to do with your
target, her heels shade you in the sunlight, dazzled.

Drive out such powers at your peril,
alive in the woods, in the deep caves
numisma of lost light, the founders,
who gift us with skills we've remembered:
how to build walls and roof, to plant trees,
to set grain and vine — an almost common knowledge,
though unpracticed — but to winch out of dreams
the music of figures, to let body flail
in images veined to the fingertips,
to lie slack in sunlight and occupy
indolence — too much trouble by far!

Everybody quiet. One more thought for the stones.
They make a cairn over history,
its losses mulled and half-reckoned

by hunters and farmers who imagined
so many wild things, but not change.

And welcome the gods of the harvest
with tipped glass and firm mind
may they slip lightly into existence
claiming lost trails of signs
faint as moonlight half-buried
in black mud:
                How naked
our lives wear, bodiless in bedlam,
until we lose our mortal skins.

(6) Derelict

Whitened in time
like a fabulous rib,
the barn sways,
riding crested furrows.
Winds flap the tin
roofed wreck
over seas of seed,
in the clear day
the fields speak riddles
of martyred stone.
Wood marries history
of hand, eye and skull,
lost children swing
in the yard's rigging,
a bird descends
with a lying branch.
Buried uncles
fall out of the past,
from ruined cribs murmur
with cobwebbed tongues.
In the overgrown garden
the roots of a smile.
I squint at the splashed
beams between half-shut
eyes, certain the rough
wind will scatter, whatever.
The others are nowhere now.
Running like vines
between boards
they assemble in air
disappear with a trace
of bright cloth on a nail
at the top of a stair.
As the latches fall off
I stand on this only
earth, where at night

pails of fresh light
run silent
from the dark troughs of another sky.

(7) Prophecy

The stones have stopped speaking.
Old voices choked in the stream's mouth,
silence invading the fields.
We move toward another festival
with nothing to celebrate.
But a neighbour comes carrying
a salamander in a shoebox,
that fabulous beast
on star-pointed feet
making straight for the pond.
And early in April three goshawks,
darkest angels of light:
as noonday shivers burning
I and my shadow are one.

Then I welcome the elders,
minds hidden from history,
with none of our wits about them
who married their hands to the stone,
like Gauguin's exotic mint
what was bitter
refining itself in the teeth
of carnivorous man—
but rendered strictly as dream
so that each leaping figure amazes,
its colours restored in a silence
always lurking at the edges
of some great deed.
These acres are lodestone or clay
for the sculpturing memory,
a double-tongued silence
lives in each fissure of truth,
and the shrewdest farmer
rolls broken earth on his lips
for a test.

Times there will be to savour
blue dust of spaces deeper
than furrows struck by the exercised mind.
In the darkness under the trees
a woman lies down
and everything begins.

A NOTE ON THE TEXT

Some of these poems have appeared in: *Descant, Fiddlehead, The Far Point, Nebula, Northern Light, Poetry Northwest, Salt, StarLine, Tesseracts* 2, 3 and 4, *Quarry, Waves,* and *Windsor Review.*

I would like to thank Robert Powell for his strong insights and for many helpful critiques over the years, Di Gomery for taking infinite pains to ensure that I should find a pleasing design form, Michael Gnarowski for his specific expertise and long-time support, Ken and Elizabeth Finch for inspiration and much encouragement. Also the various editors of *Tesseracts,* who have published several of these poems.

The writer wishes to thank the Ontario Arts Council and Carleton University for financial support.

94

Printed by
Ateliers Graphiques Marc Veilleux Inc.
Cap-Saint-Ignace, Québec
in September 1994.